Distant Path

Poems of
William Andrew Graham
The Spanish Lake Poet

Impact Books, Inc.
Kirkwood, Missouri

Distant Path, William Andrew Graham
ISBN: 0-89228-122-7

Copyright © 1996, by William Andrew Graham

FIRST EDITION

ALL RIGHTS RESERVED,
Including the right of reproduction in whole,
or in part, in any form.

Printed in the United States of America

In Memory of Children

To each child of the earth,
Let truth be our final worth,
Having us follow God's way,
Living in His light as family,
Till rest comes judgment day.
As I chose for these two,
My children through Christ,
William Lee and Betty Lou.

CONTENTS

Acknowledgement vii
Foreword ix

When Christ Came	1
House I Live In	2
My Son, My Son	3
Little Girl	4
Stairway to Heaven	5
A Boy's Toy	6
Gifts of Love	7
Christmas Memories	8
Susan's Face	9
Harbor Lights	10
Dream Castle	11
Moment In Time	12
Grandpa's Day	13
Let the Children Know	14
George Sir George	15
Forgotten Field	16
Sandi	17
Trains Go By	18
Nicholas	19
Eagles Fly	20
A Child Is Born	21
Shared Love	22
America	23
Uncle Robert's Sleigh	24
The White House Retreat	25
Christopher's Toys	26
China Cabinet	27
Lover Man	28
Circus, O, Circus	29
Gifts of Barbara	30
The Mocking Bird	31
Christmas Boy	32
Two Little Boys	33
The Olive Tree	34
Lady	35
Pallottine Retreat	36
Cry of Anger	37
Cathedral	38
Beyond the Clouds	39
An Old Christmas Dream	40
A Special Place	41
Mary's Cross	42
An Irish Cottage	43
Open Door	44
We, The Poet	45
Door of Love	46
For Whom the Bells Toll	47
Christmas in Spanish Lake	48
Someone's Love	49
Mother's Picture	50
Heart Aches	51
Esther	52
Rebuttal to Ruth	53
Billy's Joy	54
Christmas Pass	55
The Fool Within	56
Lost in Time	57
Geisha Girl	58
Homeward Flight	59

A Fallen Leaf	60	A Toast to	
Day After Tomorrow	61	The Clan, Graham	74
Measure of Love	62	Mother's Face	75
Christmas Eve	63	Dear Dad	76
Two Yellow Roses	64	Cross to Bear	77
Wildflowers	65	Alone	78
Believe Me	66	Christmas Joy	79
Cotton Fields	67	Thanksgiving Day	80
The Window Below	68	Sisters of Pallotine	81
Fisherman	69	Our Toast	82
The Connemara		Fields of Snow	83
Pendant	70	Christmas Again	84
A Christmas Prayer	71	Distant-Path	85
Nightingale	72	The Leavings	86
Prelude to Winter	73		

Acknowledgment
Towards Others

The sun is forever shining,
Though the clouds darken its glow.
Yet remember it's love shared
That uplifts a troubled soul.

Foreword

When we live in love, no color is seen!
For He died for all lost souls
Allowing each of us to share a dream.

When Christ Came

Oh, the beauty you're apt to find almost everywhere,
If you take the time to look or care.
So much is given each and every day,
Yet most of the time so few think about this when they
    pray.
Regardless of where you may roam,
Please take the time and let yourself be known,
Whether looking at the sand dunes in the evening,
Against the sky of blue,
Or in dense forest, looking up at stars shining through.

Some day you'll know beauty can be anywhere you
    choose to live,
For this earth was to be a promised land,
To those who seek and try to understand.
We the lucky ones, that truly believe,
Find each day He plants a new seed.
That shows us wisdom through sight and sound,
Which will shape our lives,
Leading us toward His goal of wanting to share a crown.
To find a place to sit and dwell,
Knowing there's peace, and that all is well.

House I Live In

The house I live in is very special to me,
For throughout each room, I share a memory
Of loving thoughts and settings well done,
A beautiful wife, loving daughter, and my son.
So many grandchildren shared this space too,
Oh, such memories I had to share with you.
The one who chose to stay awhile,
Even when things become rough leaving one
Little to bring on a needed smile.
Yet, I will never change history, or its given time,
Allowing those memories to remain forever mine.

Although life seems empty when one lives alone
I share memories of happiness, becoming a throne!
With joy of family that must grow and depart
Sometimes leaving sad thoughts in one's heart
Yet, each time you feel sad, depressed when alone,
Think of happiness shared with a family of your own,
Be glad you have this part in life to play
While loving and giving toward each in a wondrous way.
Knowing it's nice to think of the past,
Remembering all the great loves we hoped would last.

My Son, My Son

I thought about life, and what I had won,
The Lord has blessed me, with you as my son.
I sometimes think of my glory, our days together,
Whether walking the bluffs near the old river
Or swimming in nature's lakes, or moving streams
Knowing we shared as family, all wanting things.
    My Son, My Son.
What more could a father ever care to be shown
Knowing he felt a love that was always known,
Yet it has taken me all these many long years
To see the truth in God's chosen time of grace
Causing me to seek the many joys of my tears.
Knowing they are tears of happiness and love
That allow us to become more of His seed.
A Father, A Son, what else is new in life's run?
Except thanks for following my path and sight
Allowing my prayers to be answered each night,
    My Son, My Son,
        Look what we found,
        Look what we won.

Little Girl

I know the toys have been put away
The ones that remind us of yesterday,
Offering moments somehow tender and kind
Towards life's teachings of soul and mind.
That allow certain gifts between parent and child
Maybe of some uplifting feeling once in a while.
That may seem hard to the young to fully comprehend,
Yet shared love thoughts with the family now and then
Will be with them forever, till the very end.

You now make memories with a family of your own,
Sharing many of the loves you have always known.
Remembering when you were a little girl,
Having toys to play with, or to put on display.
Yet the greatest gift of all, was given from above,
Those thoughts and feelings of family, and true love.
When saying we love you now dear, and will every day,
Because you also have shown love in your enchanting way.

We know not all children can, or even care to feel this way,
Because some have bitter pain, and moments of dismay.
Maybe many remember those terrible whippings they
      had to bear,
Thinking their parents did not really love them, or care.
Even to the point where they would not accept their imput,
Forgetting they too, could know the feelings of a broken heart.
Yet, all most children need, or even hope to ever receive
Is true love, that special gift, given by those that believe,
In faith of the Living God within and above.

Stairway to Heaven

Time has long since passed, yet memories will last
Of a stairway I built towards my Father's home
A place for most seeming unknown.
I used two round banisters, five steps up or down
In helping a little blind girl find her way around.
Who had arms that hurt and feet that were unjustly scorned
Bent out of shape to the point of unfavorable form
I asked my Lord what I might do to help this child
Overcome her terrible blemish, allowing her to smile.

He planted the thought of a stairway, one she might climb
Allowing her a step toward Heaven, at least within her mind.
I thank my Lord for His message, and still do this day
For planting the seed about her stairway as I chose to pray.
Believing my prayers would be answered, knowing I
    might say
In time it would be He alone of love blessings truly shown
Where He chose to love her deep within,
When showing her true love of spirit that will forever last
Allowing her to climb all stairways of life, again and again.

A Boy's Toy

A little boy's toy was found yesterday
It had been in the attic, hidden away
Covered by beach towels from Aunt Susan.
I only remember she was a very close kin.
Yet this brought memories of another day
When I had ridden this horse, a friend to me.
I named him Big Red, such a wondrous steed,
Upon him I would ride plateaus and plains
Searching country roads and valleys to claim
Finding him to bellow and stomp a native bawl,
Causing the mares to jump and run breathlessly
Because of his commanding call.

Maybe just to let him know they remember still,
Who had been their master, and always will.
Yet, time may pass when I choose to seek the end
Knowing most thoughts of a little boy's toy
Must cease to remain allowing him so much joy,
For God will call, having him ride to that place
Only He, The Lord, can set aside.
Allowing this little boy who took a small stick
With a piece of rope forming Big Red's mane
To share a dream, just one more dream of riding
His horse to Heaven's great hall of fame.

Gifts of Love

I could not end this day
Without sending a small gift along your way,
Showing love and beauty through flowers
That should lighten a room with lace,
Yet when I remember your beauty
They could add nothing to your charm and grace.
For your eyes of blue let me see
A choice way of life I may often heed.
Remembering sweet moments you wish me to find,
Just because I choose to be your father through time.
Yet this was a special blessing for you and I
Knowing God's rewards, are a spiritual guild.

We have found in our separation, strength to grow.
It has brought us closer together for things to sow.
Of all the true feelings we may not notice at hand,
Sometimes it's only through parting we learn to understand.
So with these wonderful feelings, let us forever care
By allowing a father and daughter some gift of love to share.

Not just tomorrow or some day near the end
When the sky will be no more, for all things shall end,
Yet love thoughts spoken between a father and a child
Will live through eternal hell, if God should allow.
So rest all who may be tired and weary,
Leave all doubts and worries in God's loving hand
Believe in truth of Spirit and its command.

Christmas Memories

It's an old fashion Christmas
From the love felt within my heart,
Having all things needed
A truth, that shall never depart.
Allowing me to sing songs of love
All year round,
Even be thankful late in the year
When frost may appear on the ground.
Knowing my Christmas joys remain dear
In memories through every day of the year.
Whether we have snow at Christmas time
Or whether the ground is dry and clear.
Seems like most folk amend themselves
Not worrying too much about toys or gifts
Laying somewhere on distant store shelves,
But share most of God's feelings abound?
That seem to be everywhere in town.

Besides, most toys I seem to recall
Were made by mom and dad,
If not, there wouldn't be any gifts at all.
For they kept materials sturdy and sound,
Like lost wheels, and good lumber often found.
Also different paints, not used sometime,
Yet needed to brighten toys at Christmas time.
For it made no difference to any of us, if toys
Were store bought or not,
Because on Christmas day, each child received
A gift, no child was ever forgot.
So thanks for my way of Christmas,
Maybe a little old fashioned, yet always with cheer
For I hope and pray throughout each year
In some childlike way of His trust
When sharing all the loves from this joy
Of Saying it's Christmas, it's Christmas again,
For every little girl and boy.

Susan's Face

Like a golden rose of Erin your face changed the room,
Giving rays of sunshine, pushing away thoughts of gloom.
Even though your eyes were seeking others somehow afar,
They showed moments of endearment, some shinning star.
I could not help but notice the joy you seemed to feel,
As you looked about, probably wondering, if this was real.
A stranger's face across the table, is what you were to me,
Yet in that one moment, we shall share a treasured memory
Knowing from one's feelings we both found a friend.
To keep the seeds of love nourished, till the earth is dry,
Then choose to work towards some heavenly new high.
When shinning in His love forever, for us who hope to see.
If two strangers across the table might change their destiny
Because of a friendly smile, a few words they found anew
When expressing feelings towards God's omnipotent view.

Harbor Lights

*Our ship was sailing through a channel
On toward the open sea,
I noticed a glow from the harbor lights
That allowed some beacon for me.
Bringing back, oh, so many memories,
Of some enduring love I used to know.
One who shared a way of life from dreams
Leaving distant embers, to sparkle an afterglow.
Still filling my eyes with thoughtful tears
From all the love shared in life,
Building memories to last throughout the years.
I thought after this time
My soul might become darkened as underground coal,
Like some magic in time its self, she had to go.*

*Why was such a terrible sickness put on display,
When most of our days were of happiness, not dismay.
Yet when I see the harbor lights, am at home again,
For I often see a face within the waters
That somehow seem to glow because of the love within,
Letting me think our love will stay true till the end.
As my ship was again sailing through the channel to sea,
My mind told me the harbor lights would always call me
In some strange way those shining lights are all I need?
Sharing once more of our love that will forever be free
As long as these harbor lights
Keep calling, calling from the sea.*

Dream Castle

Someday I'll build a castle
If only in my mind
It will not be of mud or sand
For it must last till the end of time.
I'll have so many rooms to fill
With lost souls I hope to win
By letting them know they're not alone
For in me they have a friend.

I pray each day He lets me live
To help someone with all I may give.
If not a room at least a prayer
To let them know I truly care.

So when our prayers are answered
Rooms filled throughout the land,
We shall all be known as brothers
And truly understand,
In seeking the judgment of His command.
At last we found that oneness
That has always been God's plan.

Moment In Time

Love was found that moment
Your eyes met mine,
Sharing hopes forever in time
Allowing us both this feeling
We had never felt before.
While our hearts kept beating
From rhythms seemingly galore
Having us to dance forever
Through love's enchanting score.
Finding this was a special moment
When your eyes met mine.
Allowing peace and happiness together
Remaining till moments became divine.
Knowing love through its movement
May often fade away,
Yet, it sometimes lasts forever
Building dream thoughts to display.
So if you found that special moment
When your eyes met mine,
Remember, it could last forever
Till the end of all time.

Grandpa's Day

It's Grandpa's day what more need one say
A blessing in the old fashioned way,
Letting one share some part twice in life
That of being a father, sometimes a wife,
Allowing measures in life sometimes sublime
Like the love you may have forgotten
Yet through your children was always seen.
Giving you another chance to share evermore
These lasting feelings of love galore.

Just think how lucky most of us are
Having children and grandchildren like some star,
Reaching towards heaven where You are
Like Debra, Karen, Connie, Nicholas, and Malissa Sue,
Christy, Heather, Ryan, Gary, redheaded Leeann too.
A little blond haired boy Eric, always sows joy
With his cousins Christopher, a knight, yet very coy.

Yet to me they are more than just another clone,
For they have captured my heart as my very own.
Remembering how kind my Father has been
Giving me a life to share with each and everyone
Who lets all the earth know He, too, was a Son.
Sharing love from His very own heart, enough for all!
So share Grandpa's Day, a time to reach out and allow
For he loves not only you,
But all lost souls that have ever been blue
Knowing many a young child would long to say,
"Look there's Grandpa. It's Grandpa's Day."

Let the Children Know

Let the children know
Of the coming of the Lord,
Open up your feelings
And grow in His reward.
Letting the world know
He was born in a manger,
Among the sheep and
Cattle resting there,
For they knew who their
Master was from feelings
Held in the air.

The wise men came from afar
By the light of His star,
To share a treasure abound
Of our Savior on holy ground.
They came, they saw, seeking joy
Of the Christ child,
A chosen seed offering them,
A lasting creed.

So spread the word far and near,
Allowing all to preach and hear,
His coming throughout the land
Saying they felt the touch of
God's own hand,
Offering a call to love your
Neighbor, one and all.
For Christ was born to humble thee,
Yes tell the children
Let them know through love and
Understanding they grow,
Toward that space we call Heaven
That only Christ will come to show.

George Sir George

My friend has four legs, brown eyes that shine,
I guess you might say he is my little canine.
Yet, he seeks no more than I care to share,
A moment of truth, some food and loving care.
For I guess to him, I am some humble man,
Showing enough love in my touch to comprehend.
Yet, Sir George gives much more than I conceive,
When rubbing his head against my hand, leg, or knee.

Yes, Sir George is my friend, no matter his name,
Although to many he will never bring any fame.
But to me he shall always be ever true and sublime,
Making each day a pleasure, an uplifting dream.
When he licks my hand before receiving a treat,
Letting me know that his love will always be complete
Where he would never again go out in the street.
Remembering there is danger from cars, and
      people unkind,
Because he knows I love him, this friend, my little canine.

Forgotten Field

Like flowers blooming at the edge of a forgotten field,
My thoughts of you remain honest, and for real.
Remembering faded petals, softness of cheeks evermore,
Sharing a part of life, I shall choose for all time,
Changing ones history toward moments to remain kind.
Letting others know of this story that should be told,
To never misjudge flowers that bloom in a forgotten field
Just take the beauty they offer that's so pure and real.
Knowing they are of God, and His kingdom upon high
Showing a moving gift, nourished by mother nature,
Allowing all humans to often sigh, and sometimes cry.

So just be thankful you had a chance to find the way
To these fields of endearment, on this chosen day,
Causing moments to remain sublime
At least in your heart and soul, allowing you some dream.
If only from the essence of their beauty and fragrance,
Having you believe of Eden, or it's heavenly trance.
That should enlighten this certain someone who
    came along
When seeing your beauty, found the answer to their
    love song,
Enabling him to sing of all things that he is able to yield
Even the lost roses that bloom in shallows of some
    forgotten field.

Sandi

Like some pebbles that form a beach through time,
Our closeness has allowed moments truly kind.
Even through each ones loneliness, we seem to bear,
Because we still have many love thoughts to compare.
Knowing there are special people who can comprehend,
With all this unjust madness they find now and then.
Even allowing me to notice your eyes, a soft brown,
That seem to uplift my spirit whenever you are around
Although there are moments, we're truly out of touch,
Knowing yet, that a friend's feelings, can mean so much,
For they sometimes follow sadness, as a hollow scene,
Leaving them to embrace or seek another soul's dream.

When I notice your face, or those eyes that shine,
My feelings enter a love scene, that seems ever so kind,
Believing my life is ever so full, with thoughts divine.
I thank you for these feelings, they're history in time,
A recorded message of uplifting spirit in peace and love
That shall always enhance my peace of mind.
So when ever I think of pebbles forming a beach in time
Our closeness shall grow in love thoughts divine
Allowing this special bond, to many quite uncanny?
As I hope you remember me, for I will never forget Sandi.

Trains Go By

Trains go by now, seems like they never stay,
Only using a track or two as they travel away.
Finding distant yards unkind to us as shown,
Time was, half a century ago, we made up trains
From Seventh Street to Grand,
Each person having a job to do and understand.
I miss those days at the twenty first street yard
Because it was a way of life well lived and sublime,
Yet things become indifferent, somehow unkind,
Causing many changes to come upsetting one's dream.

Making up these trains used to be our beacon call,
We felt a pride and gain in a job that was well done
When the yardmaster set the call, also future Hi-Ball,
Knowing we would do the best to see his call made
No matter the weather, be it ice, snow, or rain that day.
Then time for lunch would be had, clean up work done.
Later still it was off for the rest of the day for some?
Yet, my call, like most, will be that at the end of the line.
My retirement will offer happy days on which to dine,
Allowing all the great and loving memories to slowly die
As I sit near some railroad bed, watching trains go by.

Nicholas

A seed planted that has chosen to make its call
When coming into life to spread happiness to all,
Believing he shall touch many even though so young
Knowing his light is soft and life for him just begun
Sharing some hope and a ray of light toward mankind.
Someone who shall care to be close to all of us
I am speaking of this love in Nicholas.

Who in his own way reaches out to all mankind
Asking for help, for all the mountains he must climb,
When sharing with others, love through prayers divine.
Knowing life goes forward each and every day
In trust of God's light, that has always shown the way.
So let us gather together those that believe and trust
As we open our hearts and minds in loving prayer of
Nicholas.

Eagles Fly

*I often watch the eagles flying on high
Ever so proudly up in the sky.
I know from my feelings held within my heart
My thoughts are with them, at least in part,
Wanting the same freedom, same honorable flight
To be able to choose what is wrong or right.
Having air that is fresh now and forever
Water that is kept pure, safe for each endeavor.
Yes the eagles fly high, yet must subdue to man?
Who longs to be envious of life we cannot control
That is until it begins to darken our very soul.*

*I watch the eagles flying in the sky
Wishing upon this spirit I could always rely,
To remain free of doubt or misunderstanding
When living in a nation that calls for commanding
From that true love that allows us to remain free,
To worship and live among most as family.
Yes most of us have water that is pure and clean,
Though there are many who cannot share this dream.
Like the fish or fowl, are the eagles that fly
Longing to be free of stagnation and acids cry,
That has taken away the very life as such
Who rely upon man's way ever so much.
I pray together we shall clean the air and stream,
So the eagles, fish, all animals, and man will share
This chosen dream.*

A Child Is Born

A child was born on its given day
Such joy came my way,
Lovely hair, eyes that sparkle and shine,
Allowing thoughts of another child
Born near Christmas sharing a faith divine
For those who saw Him believed through grace
That God had allowed a light for the human race.
For He was the Christ child, Host of His own,
That would rule forever on matters to enthrone.

Yet another child was born on its given day
To live in my heart, much in the same way?
For I trust throughout life, and truly believe
As the Christ child, he, too, is blessed by thy seed,
With all the love that comes from moments shown,
Allowing him to a life that may find Your throne.
So as I sit and hold this child today,
I am truly thankful of these blessings that I see,
When letting me know, I too have a love for Thee.
As I hold this child so tenderly, upon my knee.

Shared Love

May the love you share be tender and kind,
Lasting forever, till the end of time.
Believing tomorrow will be just another day,
Where you again seek moments that are gay.
Yet, if things go wrong, and you become uptight,
Think of the loneliness of some train whistle
Crying far into the night,
Ever saying to lovers, hold on, hold on to love
Good and tight, for truth and kindness is right.
For you both accepted this when life began,
Believing love knew no doubt, seeking no end.
So remember the sound of the train whistle
Crying its loneliness far into the night,
Saying to all lovers, hold on, hold on tight.

America

America, and what She means to me,
That space within my mind that sets me free.
For I, too, have dreams and thoughts as most
Sharing in Her plan where I might choose to
boast,
Being a writer of poems, from the very soul of me!
Living here gives me that right, more or less,
To spread some of the wonder She may possess.
After you read of all the pain and strife
Most have had to endure in years past,
You will understand why I love Her so and chose
To write at last.

Some may think I do not care,
Yet with my neighbor I truly will share,
Of whatever it takes to protect this country
And to help Her grow.
Being born with freedom in all thoughts of mind
I shall never forget the intolerance of the past,
And do for Her, whatever may ensure a safe harbor
Towards peace for all time.
America, I love this land!
Believing the only way any power could take an
Upper hand,
Would be if they had the almighty scope to
Control our command.
Now you know how I must feel
About this land that's so wonderful and real,
I will fight for Her from sea to sea
That's what my love of America means to me.

Uncle Robert's Sleigh

I thought of Christmas, such a wondrous time!
When remembering the rides on Uncle Robert's sleigh.
Of course this story happened over sixty years ago,
Yet the excitement, is still felt this given day.
Whether on a frozen field of ice, or fallen snow,
We would travel on Michigan Avenue, near Virginia
    Square
Looking at the people we were passing by,
Some would wave, as we sometimes acted up, showing
    we cared.
The old open sleigh was only one horse drawn,
With big lamp lights shining, to help lighten the way
As we chose to travel around our part of town,
Seeking moments we all thought, were carefree and gay.
The lights in all the store fronts, seemed bright and fair,
Yes sometimes it was windy and cool, often terribly cold,
Yet the happiness shared from thoughts, made us very
    bold.
My many thanks to Uncle Robert, and his wondrous
    sleigh,
Knowing many a child would like to say
Yes, it's Christmas again, allowing us many thoughts of
    the mind,
Remembering yesterday, and those rides, in Uncle
    Robert's time.

The White House Retreat

*I noticed a light in the White house
As I traveled the river below,
Thinking what a lovely little chapel
A place where uplifting love should flow
Wonderful feelings when you're at peace,
Believing God's way always offers a release
Of the many tensions that come our way.
Knowing this could be a measure of joy
As one chooses to meditate and pray.*

*So I told myself as I sought the sea,
That place where rivers flow eventually?
Whether under ground or on land above
A place of peace and contentment calling me,
Wondering if I should ever again find love.*

*As I walk this path of life with contradiction
I know many, as myself, seek this chosen light
That is forever shining in the White house.
Knowing people travel by car, train, or plane,
From all over this great nation.
Seeking to share the truth in this oneness
Believing people who pray and meditate together
Find peace in these moments to understand
The true values of family, under God's command!*

Christopher's Toys

I knew today was your birthday,
You probably thought I forgot?
Yet, just look at this wonderful
Present for you, I have got.
It is Grandpa's special watch,
With a little train held in.
One that runs on a magic track,
Of which there is no end.
It also counts the seconds and
The minutes all over again,
Each time the little train runs
Around each chosen bend.

A minute has passed, it is over in time,
So we must go forward to the next
Minute, on this old railroad line.
I have thought of many gifts and toys
Believing this gift should last forever
Whether it be given to a girl or boy,
Because I gave it sharing a special pride
Of all the love a grandpa will not hide
So enjoy your birthday, and this toy
Knowing it was given you to truly enjoy,
Each time you look at Christopher's Toy.

China Cabinet

I have an old china cabinet, I look at every day,
There I notice all the gifts of toys, in a special way.
Also thinking of the love given from objects of clay,
The memories and fun of finding these gifts yesterday.
But I guess I miss mostly, the arrangements to be made,
Like putting gifts in proper settings, where they stay
Maybe how they appear to others, showing a special display.

Oh yes there is a lot of life shared from my cabinet today,
For it offers man , love thoughts, that never seem to stray.
Finding when I choose to open each glassed lined door,
Another small object hidden, may be found, a secret galore.
Like some loving gift from a friend came into view again
Bringing tears I had no way of holding within.

So I think I will just go outside, sit for a spell,
Allowing my eyes to become dry, letting yesterday die.
Yet knowing each new day may allow memories to dwell
So don't feel sorry for me when you see me cry,
When looking at this china cabinet, with treasures inside
Just think of all my happy moments allowing me to stare,
Truly being thankful for all the loves I can share.

Lover Man

Whenever you're sad and lonely
In need of a helping hand
Think of me, my darling,
For you know I'll understand.
Of all those sad, sad feelings
That come back now and then
Think of me as your lover,
Your buddy and your friend
Who dreams of you each morning
As the sun shines on the dew
That brings back those memories
Of our youthful love so true.

So think of me my darling
You know I'll understand
Someone who's been your lover,
Your buddy and your man
To share in life together
Each lonely hour you find
So come on home, my darling,
Stay till the end of time.

So think of me, my darling,
You know I'll understand,
Someone who's been your lover,
Your buddy and your man.
Who dreams of you each morning
As the sun shines on the dew
That brings back those memories
Of our youthful love so true

Circus, O, Circus
Yesterday, Now, and Tomorrow

*In thoughts of yesterday when the circus began
It must have been started by a lonely man,
Someone who was tired of hate and greed
So he trained some animals to help in his creed.
Then music was added to enlighten one's soul
Allowing most people another happiness to show,
As the clowns wore make-up to gain a needed smile
Knowing many would think them funny, others senile.
So with trained animals, who shared a trick or two
Yesterday's circus was started for me and you.*

*Now the circus is truly a modern game of chance,
Mostly unreal concepts at first glance.
Yet, if one looks at the actions of children at hand,
You will see a haunting measure of how it began.
Even with all the great high wire acts,
Unbelieving stunts, most of these actors perform
I believe it's the clowns' garb, and a trick or two
That brings all the needed joy one might subdue.*

*So even tomorrow, not knowing what life may bring
I still think it will be the clowns of the circus,
That bring most of the wanted joy, allowing one to sing.
Though I do not weigh all action on clowns alone
Knowing most acts are gratifying, and should be shown,
To allow happy moments to be granted, rewarding most
Believing any clown with talent will uplift his host.
So now I will leave you with this thought before I go,
It makes no difference what act your apt to see
Just enjoy the many pleasures any circus can truly show.
Believing yesterday, now, and tomorrow, it's
    Circus, O, Circus
That allows a wondrous feeling for all of us.*

Gifts of Barbara

Of the many flower shops I have seen
Barbara's place on Luster Road shares a dream,
From flower arrangements, to stuffed animals of fun
Yet the greatest gift to be found comes from inside,
From the warmth of the hostess, who also is your guide.
She will show many treasures some hard to comprehend
Yet she, too, is a seeker, who always seems to understand.
That there might be a card for a friend who needs to unwind,
Showing thoughts of love by sending roses of the vine.
Believing one is never enough when sharing love in life,
That may help someone through doubts or unseen strife.

Or maybe it's some animal toy for a little girl or boy,
Whatever you need you will find within
Even a gift for someone who has lost a friend.
So when you're driving up north in our part of town
Please stop at Barbara's place and shop around.
For there are new Christmas cards, a treat on hand,
Remembering the changing seasons, people place on command
Allowing a different view for each person to subdue,
Knowing once you share the magic, you'll seek gifts anew.
I hope you will be somewhat like me stopping now and then,
Seeking the hostess that is so full of love, and a friend.

The Mocking Bird

I listen to the mocking bird
And the song he cares to sing,
Wondering if he misses fallen birds
Who no longer have flight of wing.
Because of the poisoned fields and streams,
Will he become extinct too?
Like the saber tooth tiger, or dinosaur,
Or the great herds of buffalo
That used to roam the western plains.

Yet here they come to conquer or claim
Taking most profit by slaughtering game,
Believing they had the right to subdue
Not knowing, or caring about nature's rule,
Yet to the Indians, it was their way of life
But the damage was done, nothing to conceive
The white man took their habitat, causing strife.
They poisoned the water, also subduing the land,
Yet saying to one another, they had done no wrong
For the government gave them a right to command.

Yet there were some who tried to restore land
Allowing water to again to become pure,
Building from dreams on high, to forever endure.
To again be free of stagnation, or its claim
So maybe their children might succeed,
And yet share in some everlasting source of gain.
Believing as family, each and everyone
They might be forgiven for what others have done.
Knowing without each animal, we lose a modest plan
That is felt around the universe,
Showing nature's way of living this land.
So try understanding creatures other than man
Who also cares to live till God's call, or command.

Christmas Boy

I remember Christmas when I was a little boy
Sharing all love thoughts and their joy,
Of all the special blessings of Mom and Dad,
Giving most pleasures to their children
Even when times were rough, and sometimes sad.
Yet at Christmas we somehow always seemed to flare,
Finding food all over the place, and gifts so fair.
Allowing Dad to fix up all the old toys around our place
Paint them bright like new for the less fortunate,
For Dad knew on Christmas day they too needed a smile
To come upon their face,
Remembering all of God's children no matter what race
Needed this moment of love instead of unhappiness or
 disgrace.

I remember Christmas when I was a little boy,
Singing carols in the living room,
Dad playing his violin, sister playing the piano at hand.
Such joy of merriment always seemed easy to understand,
When singing in harmony, Christmas songs of His
 command.
Oh yes, I will always remember most things throughout
 life,
For it's the love within a family
That will, or should, show happiness, never undue strife.
So I will leave you with one thought, somehow right?
Wouldn't it be nice to relive those moments again of time,
When love and happiness was a way to live on Christmas
 night.
Allowing me to share all the moments of special joy
Remembering myself as a little happy boy.

Two Little Boys

Two little boys were born today
On the thirtieth of June, such a display!
Looking almost the same, as twins usually do.
Yet, different in some ways,
Knowing not all twins look the same,
Remembering Jacob's sons
Ephraim and Manasseh, in their chosen day.
Showing love through salvation of God's seed,
Allowing a family who had been separated
Through doubt and stress,
To begin a new life sharing love's omniscience.

So a blessing was truly given this day
When two little boys gave joy in a special way.
Yet, who knows if they will remain the same?
For the genes within can sometimes offer a change,
Having one follow the strong male side within
Leaving the other reclaim a mother's tender grin.
Maybe one will offer hope, the other despair,
Even though both have been given love's tender care.
Yet, let's all share in this family's joy,
Knowing two little boys were born this day
Bringing love and joy to all, in a wondrous way.

The Olive Tree

The olive tree has become shallow and bare
Having most limbs fall from unkind care,
Leaving leaves disseminate upon the earth
To be blown by winds in different directions
Having some share cover from their worth.
Some to just lay upon the earth in a heap
Waiting to be settled now and then,
Hoping there could be change or repeat.

Yes now the olive tree was totally bare?
Longing for worth it once held beyond compare,
Remembering it was once young and strong
Yet became hard when no rain chose to come along.
The rain that I am speaking of, is from God above
The main root that controls the system of love,
We sometimes forget to heed what nature sows
Showing the lack of reasoning may hollow
Anything we love, or try to help, and somehow grow.

I have always prayed for this hollow olive tree
Knowing he shall always be a distant part of me,
For I, too, am a tree of sort.
Yet, have always tried to take care of the main part,
Remembering my roots and spiritual start.
Starting each day come spring, winter, or fall,
Trying to find some answer, a reason for life at all.
If only to share my fruit, covening some for the earth
Remembering truth found, comes through honest worth.
Even the olive tree must be wise in making a stand
If it chooses to remain strong or share cover,
Over the seedlings it is given to share and command.

Lady

*It's not the color of your hair,
Or the shape your body may be in.
It's all the things you say and do
Allowing me to know you are my friend.
I find it's such a pleasure
To see you almost every day,
I even speak of you unto my God,
Whenever I chose to pray.*

*I have found your true kindness
A blessing in this life,
Where most of our moments
Are spent in peace and tranquillity
Never hardened thoughts of strife.
So I would like to say one more thing
Before I must be on my way,
I truly love you as a friend
Forever hoping, thoughts never stray.*

Pallottine Retreat

At Pallottine's retreat is where they meet
Artists of all type sharing some special treat,
Showing their gifts of love from deep within
Coming together through faith, again and again.
Uplifting one's moments of stress or doubt,
Bringing tears to some, having others to shout.
Yes, some are beginners, others have traveled far
Into some enchanting land of preeminence,
Giving of their omniscience, begot from the Lord.

So it's brushes and paint, canvas, settings galore
Start outlining your sketches of plans to explore,
Start with feelings you somehow hope to bring alive
By showing others you do have dreams to satisfy.
When leaving a cry of understanding for all to see
Not only those who gather at Pallottone's retreat,
But where all artist compromise on work to complete.
Knowing most reach far beyond what spirits offer or form
Allowing each artist from around the world sublime charm
That authentic feeling of the mind you need not spare
For all people that love, surely speak to Him through prayer.

Cry of Anger

The big guns were heard all through the night
Leaving most men in stages of unjust fright,
Having most pray for a new dawn to soon appear
Allowing each one to seek, or see, each other
Breaking the thoughts of hopelessness and fear.
Believing many young men had died that night,
No matter their prayers, or faith in God's light.
Because shells falling have no feeling at all.
They just steal away all forms of life, an endless call.
Yet, when dawn appeared some relief was to be shown
By the grace of God only a few casualties were known.

The bombs had hit mostly rocky terrain,
Causing most to suffer unjust fright or needless pain.
Less than three men were killed, a small curse on life?
Though the cost of one soul is, and was, a terrible sight
For someone lost a buddy, someone had widowed a wife.
Will we ever cease, to learn, to live in peace of undue harm,
Have we not learned to make that needed plow
That shall feed the world through love and uplifting charm.
So let's all pray for this day when we shall all understand
It is only through love, we can, and must! trust in His
    command.

Cathedral

I saw a great cathedral among some tall oak trees
With lights shining bright and caressing the breeze,
There I heard some angels sing a lovely song
Being a God-fearing man, I chose to sing along
The words just came, I really don't know why.
I also felt at ease, yet began to cry.

My mind drifted forward, not behind.
Upon a large seat I saw a light as the morning sun,
I fell upon my knees in prayer
Somehow misguided, wondering why I was there.
A voice spoke, saying I had found the way,
Now be ready for judgment of what I must say.

I have noticed your life through given time,
Knowing all that suffer will not stay blind.
They will find some rest, where upon waking
To share in My everlasting vine
Telling them of no more worries or undue pain,
For in the Book of Life I have chosen their name.
So come my children and follow me.
To My chosen hill where through time all are free.

Beyond the Clouds

The light is always shining
No matter where you go,
It can only be darkened by
Each one's heart, mind, and soul.
The light that I am speaking of
Is within your memory bank,
Put there from joy of love in life
That will never dimmer or lose rank.
Because it is held there from faith
Our guidance of long ago,
Always growing each and every year
Allowing all joys of love to unfold.

Believing this light will forever shine
Not just now and then,
Yet all through eternity, till the end.
So open your heart and mind as well
As you look towards this heaven above,
Try reaching far beyond the clouds
To find that door of love
Guiding you there, never more to roam,
Believing the peace and joy you find
Will be your future home

An Old Christmas Dream

Snow kept falling, leaving the ground white and clean,
Returning thoughts of an old Christmas dream
When trees never needed the lights of man
To spread joy throughout the land.
Our moon would stay full, brightening up the night,
Allowing all joys of love toward mind and sight.

Being humble and a God-fearing man
I thought of Jesus with Mary in Bethlehem,
Also thinking of God on high.
Looking where His Son would lay in a bed of straw,
That place seen by kings and shepherds who came to call.

Some thinking of all the pain and suffering He shall command
Being the Christ child, Kind of kings, the hope for every man.
The order in which he must die, fulfilling the prophets,
A given test, since long-written, telling there shall be no rest
Though He shall leave, Yet return!
Before a single soul will ever understand,
Why He shed so much love for His fellow man.

A Special Place

*I hope you find that special place
Where moments are tender and kind,
Maybe a place held in memory
In the depth of each and every mind.
A lovely garden or some enchanting room
To relive choice moments of love in bloom,
Bringing back thoughts that thrilled so,
Yet, wondering why it has taken so long
To discover the secret your heart must know.
Even the flowers with their freshness abound
Should allow ones heart
To rekindle, love's gained on enchanting ground.*

*So I hope you find your special place
Truly among life's gold,
Believing its magic will allow your love to grow.
I know life can be short, or sometimes unkind,
Yet, if you find your special place,
Love thoughts could somehow seem to climb.
Allowing you to live in spirit and grace.
So stop and look, there is magic everywhere.
Just think how lovely and beautiful it is
In most things you see or care to share.
Believing most have found their special place
For we all know it is held within one's mind,
When they look at each with love and kindness
Believing it has the strength
Of truth and His spirit on which to dine.*

Mary's Cross

The cross that came from Mexico today
Was sent from a love divine,
By a couple of wonderful friends I met
In Ireland somewhere back in time.
I will never forget the love showed each and every hour,
Allowing my thoughts to grow like a young and tender
>*flower.*
For the rest of life, I'll forever be thinking of you,
And of all the true love you both showed, through and
>*through!*

It's the people like you that make life such a joy,
Whether spoken by a girl or boy.
You show so much from life within,
By trusting most as if they were a true friend.

I thank you for this silver cross divine,
Forever it shall be Mary's Cross of time.
When a few people met somewhere in life,
And on a trust we all cared to dine.
Writing from the love in my heart,
I hope I choose the proper words to say,
Knowing you both as I do, I think I'll just pray.
That you always find your golden charms,
Allowing to stay forever, in each other's arms.

An Irish Cottage

*Just a little Irish Cottage
Is the best I can do,
To show a place to dream about
That is for the likes of you.
Even though its only a picture
On a small white card,
It shares my love feelings within,
With uplifting thoughts of the Lord.
So look at this little Irish cottage
Within its chosen field of green,
Close your eyes just once more
To share again, some lovely dream.*

Open Door

The door is always open,
Yet, it's you who must walk through.
You can not think about life too long,
For time will pass by you.
If these feelings you will not hide,
Open your arms and let me inside.
To cherish the warmth I know is there,
The love and tenderness, yet says, beware!

This love you seek will not be blind,
And shall last forever, till the end of time.
So let this door stay open,
At least till I get through.
For I want to spend the rest of life,
Loving and being with you.

We, The Poet

*What is a poet, what must he have done?
To show the world he, too, is a son
Someone also who looks for respect for his job
That must encourage others to notice what they
Have won.
For he writes of all things in life,
Yet where is his reward most seem to dwell in strife.
I have noticed poems in magazines that win money and
All sorts of things,
Though I don't believe or agree in slang and unkind
      word
Sometimes those that judge, I wish could be seen not
      heard.*

*For I know not where their minds must lay,
In judgment of poetry that often wins being unkind
And has little or nothing to say.
Leaving most poets think these judges are very cruel,
Overlooking the heart and soul
Of us who must always write and choose truth for poetry
Through and through.
Believing all great poetry is to be judged and let go
Not being helped from those you might know,
Yet by true writings, that special gift of body and soul.*

Door of Love

There's just a light touch of love, that is for now.
That allows me to think of you, or sometimes smile.
Although in time to come, who's to say when?
This smile may blossom from enter love thoughts
Having me laugh at myself now and then or even grin.
After the opening of a new door that had been shut to me,
Because of the brightness of each day's sun
Yet telling me there is still so much in life to be won.

So please don't just stand there and think of what could be,
Help open this new door in life that will set us both free
To hold each close and kiss so very tenderly.
Believing this is what we desire from each and need.

For life only begins when two hearts care to be in time,
Looking for certain feelings and vibrations
That must come from rhythms or tunes that somehow rhyme.
Allowing us both to come from the darkness into the sun
Showing a dual light that chose to shine forever as one.

Believing it is through suffering, our unearned shame
That anyone is allowed to again capture our somehow claim,
Any of the truths are strengths from love's spirit galore
Allowing them the enchantment to again open love's door.

For Whom the Bells Toll

I hear the church bells ringing
Yet the children cry,
Knowing not all is well
For so many of the young die.
I wonder what is wrong with most
Have they forgot our spiritual host?
Why do wars keep happening?
Must we always live in sin?
Seem like most lost their reasoning
Leaving only doubts or fears
I pray all ask forgiveness
Starting different than what now appears.

For whom the bells toll
Ask those lost souls that know
From crying out their sickness,
Or death, that suffering can show.
Come, sweet Jesus, show the way
Have us, as children, kneel to pray
Asking forgiveness of our sins
Allowing us to go forward for rebirth
As when life begins,
Sharing no fear or anger or lust
Only living together as family
Where though love we find trust.

For whom the bells toll
Let it be for each and everyone
Believing through Your loving grace
All people overcome,
Reaching heights far beyond the sun.
I think within my heart I somehow know
It's the cry of understanding
That only faith in God will truly show
For whom the bells toll
Is as forthright as the seed you sow.

Christmas in Spanish Lake

I thought of our first Christmas in Spanish Lake
So full of wonderment, as one might anticipate,
Having a new home, a lovely room for each child
Offering a special blessing, allowing all to smile.
Knowing from the past, our children will share a treat,
Having a yard to play in, instead of the alley or street.
Also a live Christmas tree, with shining lights galore,
Tinsel and popcorn strung all around, old cards and more.
Bringing memories out of the past, seeming of long ago,
Yet, we look forward, through moments of love, to again sow.

I will always remember the first Christmas in Spanish
    Lake,
Knowing time goes by to the point where one reevaluates.
For the children have long since gone, Mothers in Spirit?
Yet, when that time of the year comes around again,
I put up my Christmas tree, dress it tenderly, and stare at it
Remembering the first Christmas we shared in Spanish
Lake,
Believing, finding this home was a rare and special treat,
Where our children felt safe in the yard, out of the street.
So have a Merry Christmas, try thinking of your moments
    of glee,
Sharing your life as family, as you dress up your Christmas
    tree.

Someone's Love

*Someday, I'll find that someone
My heart's been searching for,
Someone to love and be with,
Sharing dreams of the morning star.
When building some life together
In sunshine or each evening's charm
Erasing the lonely nights forever
As we kiss and lay arm in arm
Knowing life can be rewarding
From the love we share each day
Someday, I'll find that someone
Never again will I choose to stray.*

*Believing she could also be looking
For someone who is true and kind
Another to share of moments ever sublime
To erase the lonely feelings she's felt
So very long
Allowing these two someones to sing
Their own love song
To bring back all the sweet moments
When life was young and gay
Having two hearts beating happy
Showing the world of love's display.*

Mother's Picture

*I look at a picture of Mother when she was young and gay
Such love she possessed, and beauty remembered this day,
Though I could have never known of her love when life began
Yet, I was someday to be her son, held deep within.
Allowing a given time for birth and another start
From the separation of mother's cord, yet still held in part.
For life goes on between mother and child seeking to understand
Though I never noticed her looks, I thought of her loving command.
Now she has found some rest in chosen earth,
Yet while I look at her picture trying my best to think of her worth
Wondering what anyone could do even if they tried to repay,
All the love and kindness a mother gives, and puts on display.*

*I always tried to do what my mother would have me do
Believing through life what is taught by the golden rule.
For she taught in our home a place of truth and love
Where we often sang unto the Lord of His chosen light above,
Bringing all joys we had to share
When being with mother and dad, and this family that seemed to care.
So as we notice mother's picture of youth so sweet and kind
Showing a lady from the past, long before our given time,
I would like to pray for all mothers, whatever their shape or form
May God always bless you, giving of His strength and charm.
Letting all of you know, you're a queen after His heart,
For it's seeds planted through you, that allows life a new start.*

Heart Aches

Why, dear heart, did you pick this one?
She's younger than I, taller than some.
Her eyes are green, yet mine are blue,
But somehow I see all the love that's shining through.
I've felt her touch, still smell the fragrance of her hair,
Leaving thoughts I would never share.
Is this real love, or do I seek some affair?
Please let my mind know, if I am in love and truly care.

I can't sleep or forget her face,
Still from thoughts, I feel some disgrace.
I wish I knew if I had a chance,
To give all my love toward this romance,
Or just be kind, letting her go.
For someone else, well, maybe so?
Yet what is age, when love comes through.
Allowing two hearts forever to walk hand in hand,
Living with such happiness as only we may understand.

Esther

Esther, Oh Esther, why don't you hear my call?
I am not a stranger,
I am your brother, yet you hear not at all.
I have cried and cried all life through
Searching and reaching out towards you,
Yet a sister's love I have never known
Why, Oh why, has this love never been shown?
Was there something I did as a little boy?
Did I mistreat you, or act unkind,
Making fun of you like some unwanted toy?
Was it privacy that you so often sought?
Yet having brothers about, privacy was naught.

Is this that reason you left while you were young
Leaving my sister's song never to be sung,
I hope someday we shall find that proper time
Where you and I will have moments on which to dine,
So I may let you know I love you still
And, as your brother, always will.
Just remember I have felt this love since life began
Each day reliving a part that I care to understand.
So think of me as your brother every now and then
For I shall remember my sister, with love till the end.

Rebuttal to Ruth

What else can be said after such warmth has been made known,
You are truly a poet, of this I have seeming been shown.
Leaving your eyes sparkle so intense
With a voice sounding happy,
From the first moment of your comments.
Telling me you were someone special!
And of your supervisory thoughts there could be no end.

Your Christmas poem was supersensitive
When told of family and happiness within.
Having most things shared so complete
Even thoughts of the tree so admirably trim.
Yet, the greatest thing I found of the toast in words today
Is that we have found in each, a personal friend,
Who thinks of things of life almost in the same way.

So with these thoughts that must come from help above
I send to Ruth, Edward, and Family,
The best of things in life always with love.
As this light shines from far away sharing such warmth
On Christmas Day I wish the best for You and Him,
To dwell forever on some loving hymn
That will award strength to reach a special door
The door we all must be searching evermore.
Where love, peace, and compassion might well be,
By keeping the faith that allows us to stay of His seed.

Billy's Joy

The letter you mailed was received today,
Such joy and merriment had come my way.
If only you could know how my heart must feel,
Because of this truth and your picture so alive and real.
I choose to write in lines that seem an omen,
Showing from deep within this letter it is more than a poem.
So please bear with me by giving me a chance,
To prove from my heart we shall have some romance.
From truth and kindness to last all winter long,
Maybe till hell freezes over, and we both might write a
      song.

What I am trying to say and I believe you should know,
I find you a beautiful lady with a certain glow.
So take this love I offer, please don't allow it to stray,
Although life may seem indifferent I will try and find a
      way.
To put this dream together somewhere along life's road,
Having you to remember in this letter you have been told.
So allow me to say once more before I lose my mind,
I truly think of you very often
Since that first day our eyes were to entwine.

Christmas Pass

There is a Christmas pass that leads down memory lane,
I often find myself on this trail where thoughts remain.
Of all the loves through family I choose to share,
Even those troubled moments that sometimes seemed to
*   flare.*
Yet we shared most problems together for we somehow
*   knew,*
Each day was meant for living, a chapter that was new.
Yet allowing us to remember our Christmas pass,
And of all the loving kindness that would forever last.

Allowing once more for all to truly understand,
When sharing or thinking together
Most if not all problems can be solved at hand.
So we might keep on sharing in this certain dream,
Remembering those happy days when love was supreme.
We chose to walk together some Christmas path or lane,
Knowing from within our hearts all trails remain the same.
So stay with me forever in thoughts that will always last,
As we walked hand and hand together, reliving a
Christmas pass.

The Fool Within

I sometimes fight the fool within
Knowing he becomes part of me now and then.
Saying things that hurt those I love
Having me forget all that has been taught
About Him above.
Where I might forget to pray, or use the excuse
When I say I'm sorry, I was unkind with words
That should have never entered my mind.

Forgive me. I don't mean to be like you know who
That evil person within.
Who sometimes speaks out knowing I can be the fool.
Yet the hurt is done leaving me feel quite alone
Hoping you'll forgive me and let me make atone
By saying I love you.
Please forgive the fool within
Who often speaks out from all of us now and then.

Lost in Time

Some day after I have been gone,
Will you still think you were right
Not singing my song
When I offered you my heart and soul
Toward a life together that only we
Might behold.
Sharing moments in love
With our remaining time on earth.
Being content forever with what it
Could have been worth,
Even letting you find what you
Thought you had lost in a given dream?
Or even maybe a greater love, sublime.

Yet, you chose to go toward another end,
Not thinking my love of proper blend.
But age is not always felt the same,
Leaving some to grow old early in life's game.
Finding youth is often like the wind
Coming and going in all directions,
Not knowing which way to settle
Or lay its claim.
Yet a mature heart knows the way of life.
Giving moments of tenderness,
Never worry about sadness or strife.

Even tall grasses in meadows, or plateaus,
Look toward nature for their chosen rain,
Although I am no longer here, for my place
Is of naught?
I wonder if you might like to change
That moment in time,
Where you might now state a claim.
Believing you could have found a love
If you had only thought more of my heart's
Enchanting climb,
Towards God's Heaven, and everlasting vine.

Geisha Girl

*Dear little Geisha girl, how was your stay
In this distant land, knowing home is far away?
Did someone show you off as the lady you could be?
Or did he keep you for himself, needlessly?
You are so pretty, and truly made up,
I would like to drink from your slipper
Instead of this cup.
For my cup runs over with love from my heart,
Seeing a lady as you,
I will find it hard to leave, or depart.*

*Yet I know when tea has been served,
And I have had my fill
My thoughts of a little Geisha girl
May have me blend into her will.
For I have fell in love with her,
This girl from over there.
Who has jet black hair, skin lovely and fair.*

*So what may I say to someone lovely as you
Except in dreams I share a thought or two,
Remembering a little Geisha girl sweet and true.
Leaving chosen dreams that say, beware,
Yet making me happy because of thoughts
From moments we chose to share.*

Homeward Flight

We left for America, a land so great and true,
That should be loved by most not only me and you.
Yet most people I find at hand never think quite like us,
Who are from this great and wonderful land.
They're only jealous of the freedom we seem to possess,
Never thinking of all the hard work and unrest,
There must be.
Before we can think of America as the land of the free.

Those of us who must labor in some way or another,
In order to help the less fortunate on this earth,
By being God-fearing people. Knowing Her worth.
And that nothing comes easy,
Unless the reason can be of love, or its understanding
Of those in need.
For most in this great land have hopes and dreams
Of what they hope also to achieve.

So open your hearts with love, you people that hate us so,
Be thankful our hearts are not dull, or without love.
For toward most we always seem to grow,
If you believe as the Statue of Liberty states;
"Come all that are hungry and seeking a place of rest",
Try understanding America and I am sure she'll do her
    best.
She demands no more than she may give,
Just her love and kindness for all people that live.

A Fallen Leaf

A loving leaf has fallen today
It disturbed my heart in a special way,
Watching this unkind change on display.
There upon cold, cold, ground
Having one do nothing, yet try to understand,
Believing this is a cost to comprehend.
Like seeds that die of frost.
A leaf has fallen allowing me to share
Knowing my heart still grieves,
Remembering another love truly beyond compare.

Yet, I choose to write of one who has been nigh
Though lying beneath the earth still,
A brother for whom I cry.
Having thoughts remain about life on earth
Of the living kindness and wondrous joy
In all his true value of noticeable worth.
Yes, a loving leaf has fallen today,
What shall be remembered of this I say
Knowing no better love can anyone care to show
Toward a man as a brother
Knowing through his life, he, too, cared to sow.

Day After Tomorrow

*When driving this land over, from New York to the
    Frisco Bay,*
*Most things I've seen and done might make most go
    astray.*
Where so many live for each given day,
Not quite understanding why they choose not to pray.
For they see; so much for them, and nothing for others,
*Yet many churches preach, we should treat all men
    as brothers.*

I am sorry to say, it just isn't that way.
Because there are those that hate and will not try.
*In understanding, some shall live, while others
    must die.*
Thinking it's better to live without faith known,
Than to try and share with others, things shown.

Believing when two become one,
Nothing on earth seems to go undone.
Remembering all joys a family may bring,
Having love to share from Father toward Son.
That helpful hand that should come to everyone,
Letting us be sure of true faith,
Of which some day will surely come!

Measure of Love

*How do you measure a tear drop
That comes from a crying eye?
Brought on by thoughts and emotions
That somehow will not die.
Like the love of some child saying
I love you, mother and dad,
Let us share some happiness this day.
What has happened to move this child
Crying from loneliness, yet trying to smile.
What have we done causing this shame,
We see it where we work and upon the street,
Even among neighbors, we should love and claim
As sisters and brothers, whenever we meet.*

*Yet, they, too, show this harm that comes from
Unkind feelings and doubtful emotions,
That allow greed and lust to cause our separation
From true love and devotion.
Knowing from within we must show the way
Erasing the lonely thoughts of every child,
By showing true love between mother and dad
Allowing only this picture to be on display.*

*How do you measure a cup of loving joy,
That may come from a little girl or boy?
Just open your heart and mind to excel,
Seeking moments of peace that history will tell
As you look through eyes of love from above.
So how do you measure a tear drop
That may fall from some crying eye?
You share these moments when love is king
To last forever, and on this thought you rely.*

Christmas Eve

It was Christmas Eve, yet no snow on the ground.
I arrived at my daughter's house
To exchange gifts with all the family around.
A thoughtful house so clean and neat,
Food of abundance, such a treat.
The joy of children singing in song,
Enlightenment to one and all, who cared to sing along.
Trying to guess what there could be,
When shaking each box, or gift in some moment of glee.
Yet the greatest gift I found from this house within,
Was all the loving happiness, and never-ending grin.

After having such a treat from food and drink,
The gifts rewarded to all in our family link.
I chose to leave, yet with some regret,
Although knowing arrangements had been made
With others I had met.
And upon leaving from my daughter's house,
There in the cold where they must have stood
I heard these voices saying we love you, we love you,
And hold so many thoughts dear, as only we could.
I started to drive away with a fallen tear in my eye,
Remembering thoughts of someone else, and God on high
Letting me know of things I had hoped to see,
So I could go on toward another loving Christmas Eve.

Two Yellow Roses

There are two yellow roses in a setting well done,
Placed upon the book of life
Where a joyous picture of peace and faith should come.
Through the beauty of nature ensuring of God's might
With all the sights of wonderment,
As most may choose to read of Scriptures delight.
Allowing all these moments towards nourishment of
Each one's soul,
No matter the temptation of where you are apt to go.

This picture of two yellow roses on God's book of life
Will stay within your mind through all doubt or strife.
Even when you feel dreary from troubles of your mind
Think of these two yellow roses upon God's book of life,
Look through the Scriptures that have helped in time
From one who was lonely in need of His mighty hand,
After reading and thinking things over, you'll comprehend
That it is only through faith, we might learn to understand.

Wildflowers

In the fall of the year when wildflowers appear,
I nourish the beauty of nature that is quite clear
Knowing summer will come and sing her song
Leaving my time of the year to come along.
As I choose to pick wildflowers that always grow,
For they last all winter long resting under the snow.
To give and share beautiful memories like I have of you
Knowing all the time a parting of life was overdue.
Yet, in each and every fall a bouquet of wildflowers
    appears,
Leaving me to remember that spring was here with
    daffodils
Though wildflowers I pick give me my greatest thrill.

For they remain very dear to me,
These colorful flowers of love, a departed seed.
Allowing a gifted treasure in life each and every fall
Giving a harvest to all that look at nature
Believing every season shares some moments of awe.
So whether in spring, summer, autumn, or fall,
There is a need for everyone to make this call
To pick daises, daffodils, or some red roses on a hill,
Yet, my choice will always be to pick wildflowers
That come in fall, lasting the whole winter long.
Allowing me each year to sing my song.

Believe Me

Why did you ask me if I felt different today,
Were you not happy with what I had to say?
You know I love you, for I have told you so.
Why must I prove myself,
Or act like some untruthful gigolo?

If you don't know my feelings are fair,
I wish you would leave, or just get out of here.
I've tried to show my heart, always staying close,
Instead of far apart.
Yet what must I do to keep your love?
Act like some curio or cooing dove.

Why don't you let me be myself,
That fellow you married and chose to love,
Who could have never been kept on some shelf.
So stop all that fuss, get over here.
Let me kiss you, and hold you, forever, my dear.

Cotton Fields

I remember when I was just a young boy
Playing in cotton fields, seeking some joy,
Though most of the time just dragging a sack
Trying to pick cotton, most times just an act.
Knowing Mom and Dad had this job most every day
Even when times seemed ever so hard,
They still shared their love in a special way.
I often think of our worn out old blue jeans
Vinegar used on swollen and cut fingers,
Sometimes bleeding, causing many of us to scream.

Yet, there where times after the harvest was done,
We would gather for a picnic, such a place of fun.
People would dance or sing, sharing new thoughts
Erasing the hurts and strain of lower back pain.
Caused from hours of bending, sharing a modest gain,
Knowing later, chopping in the fields must be done,
Then the clean up work, getting ready for the rerun.

Till then we shared some enjoying moments at hand,
By living near our neighbor, from love of God's
    command.
Knowing after the picnic was over, trash all cleaned up,
We might just look at our family remembering this cup,
Yet not forgetting the general store, or bills to pay
Maybe a dollar or two from wages earned that day,
For cash was hard to come by, very short, at times unkind.
Now you know a few things about my life as a young boy
Helping Mom and Dad pick cotton, searching for some joy.

The Window Below

There's a light flickering from the window below
Leaving me to find within myself a fear to sow,
Where at times I feel mad, almost insane
From this place where I dwell, and its terrible shame.
Not knowing or believing I might find some force
To deliver me from this hell or its unworthy source.

I've asked for help in so many prayers
Yet, has my mind really sought to find some rest?
To allow peace, or is this just the start of a test,
Like so many other poets or saints from the past
Wherein they must live by faith, waiting Your call?
Believing that freedom might come at last.

Then maybe, I will find a place in which to dwell,
Where all the love and peace I have longed for
Will enlighten or tell of the very heights of heaven
A place I have always hoped to find,
Since I was a little boy and heard of your living vine.

Fisherman

I feel so happy, seems as though I have found my way,
Where life has been kind from unknown sights not seen.
To let me know that all things are not made of clay,
Though I should fall yet not away from the main stream
Even though the road is rough, man is of a dual team.
You tell of this in most Scripture I read,
Allowing me thoughts that are truth and of need.
Some men are to remain fishermen, of this I would cling.
That is why I am so happy I have found my way to sing
For it's up and forward I choose to go,
Knowing from within my heart there was always a glow.

Where I would go among men and women alike to sing of
The sacred ark,
Enhancing most souls to pray together
Where they may never again care to depart.
As they were chosen people to start life over again,
Spreading true life where love, peace, and happiness
Will always find a way in which to somehow blend.
Because of my love thoughts held within,
These dreams of being a fisherman will never end.
Having me sing and shout each given day
Knowing I have never gave up as others who chose to
      give in.

Believing in truth and Your light of love that always wins
      out,
Allowing me to go among women and men and somehow
      shout
The Lord is King and will be here each and every night.
So please stay and listen for it is of Him that we are about.
No man is to be a mountain for he is to be a valley between
Yet all he must ever do is look up into God's Heaven,
Then he shall forever be seen.

The Connemara Pendant
Written by my soul mate, Ruth Newton Mattos,
For whom I shall always be grateful

This stone from Connemara
That means so much to me
For all the lore it represents
In Irish history,
Enchants me with it's soft green hues
It's many varied tones,
Suggesting once a molten state
Embraced ancestral bones.

I see the blood of Ireland
Immersed in depths of jade,
Blood lost defending home and hearth
In ancient forest glade.
The lighter spots I see as tears
Whose briny taste is known
Full well to wives and mothers
Through long centuries of moan.

Oh, Ireland, the heart of you
The soul of you, implores
Response from scion of those fled
To strange and distant shores.
For those uniquely Irish
Inherent in Your spawn
Is bound forever by the ties
That from Your roots are drawn.

A Christmas Prayer

*Merry Christmas and happy New Year
To each and every one,
Let us share from the seeds of love
As the Father unto His Son.
By living each day of rewards not shown.
Maybe the prayers of strangers spoken
Yet to most unknown.
Believing all men are to be brothers
Yet fail to understand,
All they need do is think or live
In faith of His uplifting command.*

*Please look through your eyes as children
With no shame or undue hate,
Allowing all people who live upon this earth
Some peace and happiness, before it's too late.
So take this love that has been offered,
Throw it into the oncoming wind
Believing it shall bring a measure of truth
For all lost souls to live and love again.
So let's wish a merry Christmas
To each and every one,
Believing this New Year can fulfill hearts of love
As the Father unto His Son.*

Nightingale

There is a lady of the evening who walks with pride,
Leaving all things open for those with things to hide.
Like seeking her company sometime,
Maybe just to talk or release emotions of their mind.
Believing they are unable to talk to wives at home,
Thinking maybe a stranger might enlighten troubles sown.
Oh yes, there are ladies of the evening who walk with pride,
Remembering the hurt and undo shame
Yet listen to the woes of others, and the twilight of age,
With the doubt and stress of moments unknown
Allowing her to become less than noble, upon this stage.

Yet the ladies of the evening seem to always touch others,
By listening to their troubles, trying to undo the hurt
Between these fathers, mothers, sisters or brothers.
Always hoping she might find some answer from deep
        inside,
Allowing her to still look at all people
And forever believe she has the right to walk with pride.
Knowing she had taken the time to listen to their troubles
Yet did not laugh at them, or try to hide.
So if you meet some lady of the evening, do not shame her,
She might be that certain someone that listened with pride
As she uplifted your feelings of love, from deep inside.

Prelude to Winter

Leaves keep falling, turning a golden brown,
Winter draws near, as frost lies upon the ground.
So little left of Autumn, a time to wonder,
Leaving my mind with untold thoughts to ponder.
About all the color that seems to appear,
In mother nature's changing each year,
Allowing us another sober look, at what we may win
A time to sit and think,
What she has to offer us in each and every link.

Like the sky that shows many shades of gray,
Also white caps drifting around a sea of blue
Letting our minds drift towards dreams we subdue.
Yet, winter can be unkind, with dying leaves and
Trees that become bare, a sight one must share,
Even lightning strikes the likes of trees, forests burn,
Animals die, leaving land that's charred and unfair.
Torrential rains come mixing with the burnt soot below,
Fertilizing the land for seeds windblown, to sow.

Most forget mother nature is of God upon this earth,
Having that command to show us, His trust, of her worth,
Showing us the good she may allow as well as the bad,
Never letting us forget all the blessings we have had.
So winter comes, as days seem long, with the cold of
*   snow,*
Just bundle up the thoughts of love, from spring's
*   afterglow*
Knowing we must live our lives for many different
*   reasons*
Forever looking towards peace of mind in each and all
*   seasons.*

A Toast to the Clan, Graham

*To the clan Graham
I would like to say,
We have shared a kindness
That shall always be on display.
Knowing no matter where we are
Apt to go,
In Scotland we shared some seeds
To truly sow.
Of love and kindness, with joy in
Between,
For in each heart and soul we
Have shared a dream.
I am thankful to each one who
Helped me find inspiration to
Write this toast.
May the soft winds of love
Forever be at your endeavor,
To push you toward His kingdom
Where true love lives forever!*

Mother's Face

*My eyes opened up by a voice I choose to hear,
Such a lovely face began to appear
Knowing there's a love I've been long inside,
Held by a cord of life, somehow tied.
Giving my body the strength it would need,
For God had granted another life from His seed.
Showing all the love I might feel now and then
Towards mother's care, and ever-loving grin.
For at feeding time I must nurse a drink of life
That only she may give, because of life within.*

*As I drink my fill, still watching her
I just lay unmovable, not so much as a stir,
Allowing this small brain, I may conceive
Such wanting love between mother and child,
Who has lived this day only a short while.*

*Yet, I think of all the love that surely must come
When I become older, and say, look Mom, look
    at me
I'm here, your little boy, your loving son.
So now I will close my eyes to find some rest,
Because in life I have been given this test.
Yet, please let me see a picture, not of satin or
lace
But the love and tenderness of my mother's face.*

Dear Dad

I have always noticed the blue of your eyes
And the light from the grayness of your hair,
Never forgetting why things of life, at times
Seemed unfair.
Knowing cuts on your hands, often dry and bare
Were from working outside, no warmth or cover there,
Yet I hardly ever heard you complain
Unless it was of days when we seem to have had too
Much rain.
Always taking life as it is given, each and every day,
Accepting whatever the Lord chose to put on display.

I would just like for you to know that I have
Always been glad,
That our Lord chose for me such a wonderful dad.
Who shared each day, and the night times too,
Letting all in the family know of his love
By showing his feelings through and through.
I always felt you were a humble man
When choosing to live by rules made right,
Somehow living as your Father, who kept thy sight.
Believing in truth and light toward family love
Knowing you would go on to sing God's song above.

For throughout life and memories lingering on
I, your son, want to thank you dad,
Even though life for you has since long gone.
Yet I sometimes think, almost any given day,
Of this loving family of my own, for I often pray!
Hoping they will find in me love and truth of a humble man,
To also guide them toward that chosen light
Which lets all souls live to love and understand.
Believing we can all remain happy or chose to be sad,
Somehow I find happiness and contentment to remain
Near, or with, my special dad.

Cross to Bear

Each day I find a cross to bear,
Believing Christ chose to be there
To wash my sins and show the way
I should live my life, each and every day.
For Satan steals, and will always try to sway,
Yet, I will not give up in what must be
Believing within my mind Christ died for me.

To give me life where I might understand,
What it means to be humble, and live as man.
By showing each day, at least in part,
A greatness some day He is apt to start
Within the very soul of me?
For in dying, He chose to plant a special seed,
So I might have life to live and grow
In all the warmth and love of His trusting care,
Because each day I find a cross to bear.

Alone

*As the sunlight shines through my window pane
It shows a new day of life I must attain,
Yet I wonder if this day will bring happiness,
Or more endless stress?
I seem to be all alone in this world, no friend.
Though hoping I might erase this terrible sin
That leaves me sad both night and day,
Even though sometimes, throughout the night I pray.
If for no other reason than to stop this pain
From so much doubt of all my endless shame.
That causes me to feel that I have always been wrong
No matter what, the music, or the joy of my song.*

*I know the story that man lives not by bread alone,
Yet, by all things taught from love truly shown.
I have tried my best throughout each night and day
But no answer ever seems to come my way.
Seems like time would let me find the friend I need
For it states in Scriptures, all men are brothers
And come from God's chosen seed.
So, I guess it's down the road, quite all alone?
Until my time of judgment upon Your throne.
Then, I will have found my chosen friend indeed!
Allowing me to sing the song my heart has known
By believing, and keeping Thy faith,
I too, will become a son, to love and always to be free.*

Christmas Joy

*May you always remember the joys of Christmas
As they are meant to be, each and every year,
Letting you know of His coming
Yet, to never be swayed from guilt, or feelings of fear.
For He shall always love you!
Even though in life we may sometimes have doubt.
Just remember of His birth.,
Believing the Lord takes care of our troubles-
By sorting them out.
To let each soul find that needed rest now and then,
When they remember He is their heavenly Father,
Savior, and always their friend.*

*So if you ever find this special blessing,
In the course of any given day,
Remember to pass these love feelings on
Towards strangers you're apt to see of dismay
Knowing God will always love you
Whether you're happy or sometimes sad.
Because in the beginning He planted all seeds
That were to become mothers, or some chosen dad*

Thanksgiving Day

Thank you, dear Lord, for this special day
Of sharing thanksgiving the old fashion way,
With all the love my heart might show
Whether with family, or with others who sow,

I have read it is by giving, that we share,
Of all the great loves in life with those
Who really care.

So with love in my heart, I thank You for this day,
Where I can ask a blessing in the old fashion way.

Sisters of Pallotine

The sisters of Pallotine in their cloth of black and white
Are all called for this special moment of light,
Some come from large cities, others from a small farm.
For each share a gift, to most of equal charm.
When helping the lonely through meditation or prayer,
Letting them know some sister will always be there.
To encourage their feelings toward God's everlasting light,
No matter the time, or the unseen temptations of the night.

Yet, the sisters have callings, as you can see?
Some are to be teachers, others work in the hospitals,
While others grow in the spirit of the gospel, seeming free?
Yet do not let this fool you,
For their hearts are always seeking the light of the Lord,
Believing in His final call.
Hoping they will be received, finding a just reward,
To be children of their Father on high
Never to wither, or lose faith and die.

Our Toast

A toast to Jim Kelly, one hell of a man!
Who has lead us into measures of happiness
That we may all learn to understand.
Allowing us to give some token,
From the love of each one's heart.
Although we all shall be saddened
For it is now time to leave and depart.

Yet your face has enlightened us
Along each and every mile,
Leaving it to show the magic of Ireland's love
With each enchanting smile.
So until we meet again, or send a line,
Thanks from all of us, till the end of time.

Cast of thirteen
Who shared an Irish dream

Margaret Kunz
Willis Kunz
Phyllis Danforth
Clarke Danforth
Ruth Bangert
Aurelia Kennedy
Marcella Fournie
Ruth Bradfield
Barbara Callan Nokes
Donna Tanburello
Shirly Dooley
Jim Kelly
Wm. Andrew Graham

Fields of Snow

The heavy snow kept falling so endlessly,
Changing my green field to look as the sea.
Except for the tall trees, that seemed to harbor above,
As a sign post, that seemed to show thoughts of you
Remembering life and all this sadness, without love
Allowing me no place to go, or sometimes roam,
Like the leaves that float across a field of snow
Bringing my thoughts to a gathering place unknown.
As the wind kept blowing and the snow kept falling
I knew life for me would offer its last calling.

That I would write of sadness, sometimes of joy,
Remembering most things that had happened as a boy.
And I also know time will come, when I care very little
If the snow will blow across the field endlessly,
Causing my green field to look, or show signs of the sea
For I know life goes on, like all seasons that must go
I, too, will disappear.
Just like the Sun will melt this chosen field of snow.

Christmas Again

Christmas will come soon, with love of heart,
A truth remembered of the Christ child born
To give each life a new start.
Some ray of hope for all mankind,
When sharing His light till the end of time.
With love in family only He may command,
By giving wisdom to all lost souls, every child,
Lady or man.
Christmas will come soon, by the joy I feel,
Allowing happiness to convene-
In love thoughts that are noble and real.
Snow flakes keep falling ever so light,
Softly, softly, throughout this Christmas night.

It's Christmas again, a time to truly be of Him
The One, who lets all souls feel a truth within,
Whether alone, or in some dark room, no place to go,
Or traveling down some country lane sharing its
After glow.
Maybe the setting of the Sun or the Moon's light
Brings all these happy faces that shine tonight,
When thinking of family and their warmth on this
Christmas day,
Knowing it is love well remembered, often held in,
That allows this happiness, when sharing of Him!

Distant-Path

All my life I have traveled a distant path,
Which has lead to pleasures, or some hidden wrath.
Because no one knows what will happen any hour,
Like sweet grapes used to ferment, often turn sour.
Giving us life of many seasons, with many ups and downs,
That will come to all who may seek this road to glory
Even for those that seek kindness, as that of the clowns.
Knowing just like the wind, blowing in all directions
Yet no one ever knows where it might settle?
My path of life may always lead me to some distant shore
To seek or try to find, what my heart is searching for.

Yet, like all of life, you'll find many places unkind,
For most find that love must come from within
So while you search distant paths seeking thoughts divine
Just remember it might be the love found in another's heart
That may be the only decent judgment, that is honest and fair,
Allowing you to share with another
Who may be also looking for some distant path or lane
Seeking your love, which may be all they need for cover.

The Leavings

I sometimes think of the leavings,
Words written of another time,
Expressing moments through feelings
I thought were thoughtful and kind.
When trying to relive days with others
I loved enough to call sisters or brothers.
For I often look through papers I put away
Knowing I might reclaim yet another day,
To look for words with loving feelings
Putting them in poems that seem to rhyme
Telling more of my thoughts for history
For a later date through time.

Yet I know the greatest feelings to behold
Are the teachings of the Lord's Scripture,
That should always live within each heart
And soul,
To enlighten One far greater than man
When seeking all things He has yet to sow,
Or ever try to understand.
So let me share some leavings from yesterday
To share in poems for all the world to read
Allowing more of God's light for us who pray.